Soft Skills Sleuths

JOB SEARCH

Investigating Life Skills Success

Diane Lindsey Reeves with Connie Hansen
Illustrations by Ruth Bennett

CHERRY LAKE PRESS

Published in the United States of America by Cherry Lake Publishing Group
Ann Arbor, Michigan
www.cherrylakepublishing.com

Created and produced by Bright Futures Press
www.brightfuturespress.com

Reading Advisor: Marla Conn, MS, Ed., Literacy specialist, Read-Ability, Inc.
Illustrator: Ruth Bennett
Cover and Page Designer: Kathy Heming
Design Elements: © mijatmijatovic/Shutterstock.com; © GoodStudio/Shutterstock.com; © Denis Cristo/Shutterstock.com; © Lorelyn Medina/Shutterstock.com; © Yaroshenko Olena/Shutterstock.com; © rangsan paidaen/Shutterstock.com

Cherry Lake Press is an imprint of Cherry Lake Publishing Group.

Library of Congress Cataloging-in-Publication Data has been filed and is available at catalog.loc.gov

Cherry Lake Publishing Group would like to acknowledge the work of the Partnership for 21st Century Learning, a Network of Battelle for Kids. Please visit http://www.battelleforkids.org/networks/p21 for more information.

Printed in the United States of America
Corporate Graphics

TABLE OF CONTENTS

What Are Soft Skills and

Skills are needed to succeed at any job you can imagine. Different jobs require different skills. Professional baseball players need good batting and catching skills. Brain surgeons need steady hands and lots of practice with a scalpel. These are examples of **hard skills** necessary to do specific jobs.

Everyone needs "**soft skills**" to succeed in life. Soft skills get personal. They are about how you behave and treat people. Soft skills are the skills you need to be the very best *you* at home, at school, and at work.

"Sounds good," you say. "But I don't have a job. Why do I need to worry about soft skills?"

Ahh, but you do have a job. In fact, you have a very important job. You are a student, and your job is to learn as much as you can. Learning soft skills makes you a better student now. It also gets you ready to succeed in any career you choose later.

This is especially true for **Job Search** skills. True, you probably aren't job hunting now. Even so, the same skills you'll need to find your dream career later can help you put your best foot forward now.

In this book, you get to be a soft skills **sleuth**. You will track down clues about what good (and not so good!) job search skills look like. You will **investigate** four job search soft skills cases about what it is like to be:

- **Curious**
- **Self-Aware**
- **Well-Groomed**
- **Prepared**

Why Do I Need Them?

HOW TO USE THIS BOOK

Here's how you can be a soft skills sleuth. In each chapter:

- **Gather the facts.** Read the description about the soft skill.
- **Read the case file.** Check out a situation where soft skills are needed.
- **Investigate the case.** Look for clues showing soft skills *successes* and soft skills *mistakes*. Keep track of the clues on a blank sheet of paper.
- **Crack the case.** Did you spot all the clues?

SOFT SKILL #1

Quick! How many different careers can you name? Five? Twenty-five? The U.S. Bureau of Labor Statistics keeps track of these things. According to this government agency, there are more than 800 categories of careers to choose from. And this doesn't include the ones that haven't been invented yet!

Choosing a career is one of the biggest decisions you'll ever make. You want to get it right! But how do you pick one out of so many? How do you even find out about all the different choices?

You get **curious**! Pay attention to what people are doing around you. The real world is full of people doing interesting jobs. Your job is to get curious—even nosy—and find out what they do. Notice people at work in your community. Ask questions about what they do. Make connections between products and the people who make them. Think beyond the obvious and try to figure out how things work.

Your curiosity will lead to many fascinating discoveries. Plus, you will get ideas for future careers that just might work for you.

Get Acquainted with the Real World

- Ask your parents and other trusted adults to tell you about their careers.
- Participate in "Take Our Daughters and Sons to Work" events and other job shadowing opportunities.
- Visit local workplaces to watch people at work.
- Read books about different types of careers.
- Use the Internet to find information about careers you are interested in.

> "When you are curious, you find lots of interesting things to do."
> —Walt Disney

CURIOUS

SOFT SKILLS CASE #1: CURIOUS

A big career fair is happening in the gym. All kinds of professionals are available to share stories about what they do. There's a police officer, doctor, baker, scientist, hairstylist, and even an animal rescue worker. Miss Garber's class is excited about this chance to find about more about all kinds of careers. It's their big chance to get inspired about all the different careers they can have someday. The only question is, which career should they explore first?

DO:
Investigate curiosity successes and mistakes!

DO NOT:
Write in this book!

It's Career Day! Some students will explore favorite or brand-new careers. Others will miss their chance to become more career-aware.

SAY HELLO TO YOUR FUTURE CAREER!

CURIOUS

The real world came to school today. Who looks curious about careers?

Did you find all the successes and MISTAKES?

Start here!

Mistake.
Stop messing around with the stuff on the exhibit table and start asking questions!

Success!
Making a good first impression with a nice, firm handshake.

Mistake.
Turn off the phone and tune in to the action around you.

CASE NOTES

How can you explore the real world?

Success! You'll never know unless you ask!

Mistake. Missing out on your chance to learn more.

Did you find them all?

Mistake. What's so funny about people trying to help you find a bright future?

Success! You'll never know if you like a career unless you give it a try.

Success! Signing up to volunteer and learn even more.

SOFT SKILL #2

How well do you know the person you look at in the mirror every morning? Maybe it's time to get acquainted! Everyone has abilities, interests, and needs. The more you know about yours, the better.

Abilities are the skills or talents needed to accomplish things. Some of these things are easy, and you can do them well. Others are more difficult, and you have to work harder with them. For instance, some people are really good at math. Others struggle with it. When choosing a career, a **self-aware** person can match their best abilities with those required for a specific job.

Interests are the things you most like to do. It's how you like to spend your time. Let's say you are good with numbers and really interested in sports. You might mix the two with a career as a sports **statistician** or as an **accountant** for a professional sports team.

While you are at it, get in touch with your needs. Your needs are tied to your feelings or emotions. For instance, what do you need to feel comfortable in a social setting? Lots of people and lots of noise? Or just a couple good friends and a fun video game?

No one looks, acts, and thinks exactly like you. Self-awareness lets you be the very best you *and* do the very best job!

Get to Know Yourself Better

- Know your strengths and weaknesses.
- Talk about how you feel.
- Try new things to encourage new interests.
- Figure out what triggers strong feelings in you.
- Ask for what you need.

"Knowing yourself is the beginning of all wisdom."
—Aristotle

SELF-AWARE

SOFT SKILLS CASE #2: SELF-AWARE

Ms. Bryan's class has been talking about self-awareness. Instead of a quiz, she asks students to show her they know what self-awareness is all about. Their assignment is to share their favorite abilities and interests with the rest of the class.

Little did she know what an interesting group of students she was teaching! Her class has lots of talent on display today. But a few students don't seem to know what to do. Which ones are showing good self-awareness skills?

DO:
Investigate self-awareness successes and mistakes!

DO NOT:
Write in this book!

Some of these students are self-aware about their interests and abilities. Some need to give it more thought. Which ones are which?

TO YOUR OWN INTERESTS BE TRUE

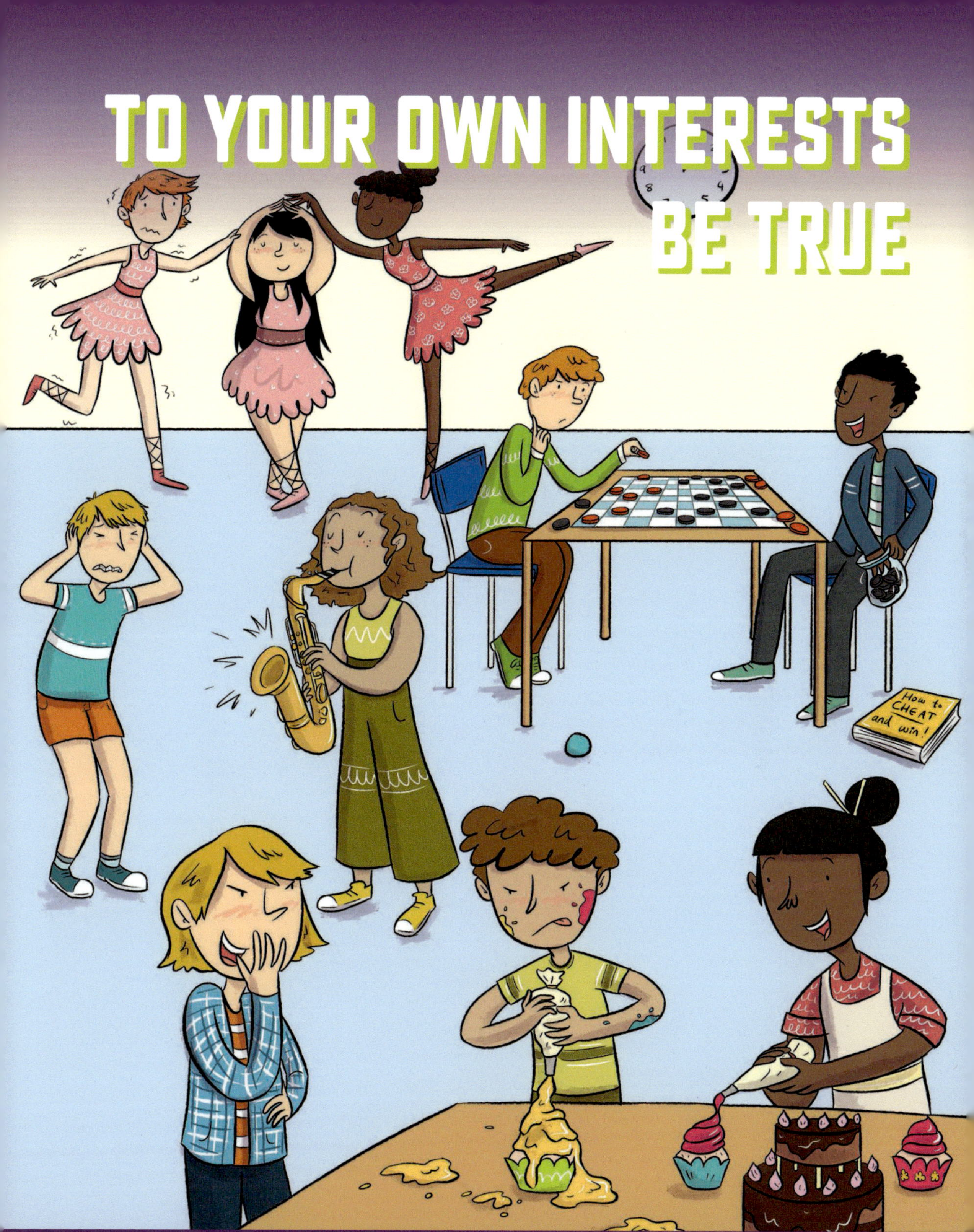

SELF-AWARE

There's lots of self-awareness going on in Ms. Bryan's class today. Who has it, and who doesn't?

Did you find all the successes and MISTAKES?

Start here!

Mistake.
One person's interest can be another person's noise.

Mistake.
If you are really interested, you won't be bored.

Success!
Applauding and encouraging the interests of others.

Mistake.
Self-awareness isn't discovered by doing nothing.

CASE NOTES

Success! All interests count!

Success! Teaching others what you know.

Say hello to you!

Did you find them all?

Mistake. Don't make fun of something unless you try it.

Success! Sharing your interests (and talents) with others.

Success! Trying new things—and if at first you don't succeed, try and try again.

SOFT SKILL #3

Everyone has a bad hair day once in a while. But having a bad hair day every day means it's time to rethink your grooming habits. Grooming includes all the things you do to look (and smell!) good. Good personal **hygiene** includes include bathing, brushing your teeth and hair, and using deodorant every day.

As a life skill, good grooming goes even further. Being **well-groomed** means dressing the part for specific situations. For instance, wearing a T-shirt and ragged jeans to a football game might be fine. But it wouldn't be a good look for attending most weddings.

Most schools and many workplaces encourage casual ways of dressing. That means you can wear comfortable clothes. You should still use good sense in choosing clothes that look good and fit well. And they should be neat and clean.

One of the first things other people notice about you is your grooming habits. If you smell bad and look like a mess, your appearance says you don't care. People get the idea that you don't think much of yourself. They may wonder if they can trust you to take pride in your work or do your best on a team. Bad grooming habits can cost you friends and opportunities.

"Dress for success" is a saying you may hear in the business world. It's good advice, because if you dress for the part, you are more likely to get the part.

How to Dress for Success

- Take a shower every day!
- Deodorant—don't leave home without it!
- Brush your teeth at least twice a day and floss every night.
- Wash, brush, and style your hair.
- Wear clean clothes.

"[You are] a walking billboard. You want to look good to everyone who is watching."
—Chandler Parsons

WELL-GROOMED

SOFT SKILLS CASE #3: WELL-GROOMED

The civics class is visiting city hall today. City hall is where local government happens. Mayor Perry is on hand to give the students a tour. This is a big deal, and the students were asked to dress in their best **business casual** attire. That means well-groomed and professional.

Some students look the part. Other students didn't seem to get the memo. Turn the page to decide which students are dressed for success at city hall.

DO:
Investigate grooming successes and mistakes!

DO NOT:
Write in this book!

WHO'S LOOKING GOOD AT CITY HALL?

Who is dressed to impress the mayor? Who needs a fashion makeover?

WELL-GROOMED

Take a look at these well-groomed students! Who needed to spend a few more minutes in front of the mirror today?

Did you find all the successes and MISTAKES?

Start here!

Success!
That spiffy necktie adds an extra professional touch.

Mistake.
Getting a whiff of that bad hygiene.

Mistake.
Bed head, pj's, and bare feet. Seriously?

Mistake.
Earth to astronaut: dress up as the best you.

CASE NOTES

Are you looking your best today?

Mistake. It's city hall, not a city pool!

Did you find them all?

Success! Now this is business casual at its best—a clean, comfortable, put-together look.

Success! Nothing like a confident handshake to seal the deal.

Success! Showing up in your best outfit shows you care.

SOFT SKILL #4

Looking to land the career of your dreams? You'll have to prove that you re the best person for the job. For most job seekers, that means being **prepared** in three ways. You'll have to fill out an **application** and submit your **resume**. Do these well and, with luck, you'll get an interview.

The application is a form you fill out in order to apply for a specific job. Employers use it to gather information about you and compare you to other applicants. It is often your first chance to make a good impression on a future employer. Follow the directions and make sure your answers are neat, complete, and honest.

A resumé is another important job-seeking tool. It is a document that sums up your **qualifications** for the job you are interested in. A resumé is your chance to sell, or market, yourself. It lists your education, experience, achievements, and skills.

If your application and resumé spark an employer's interest, then you will be invited to come in for an interview. This is your chance to meet face-to-face with the employer. This person will ask you lots of questions about your experience and your interest in the job. You will also ask your own questions about the company and what the job would be like. This is your time to shine!

When it comes to finding a job—any job—there is one rule you can count on. Come prepared or don't bother to come at all.

Get Ready to Succeed!

- Start now by working hard and getting good grades in school.
- Get involved in school organizations and clubs.
- Make sure your social media accounts reflect someone a company would want to hire.

"By failing to prepare, you are preparing to fail."
—Benjamin Franklin

PREPARED

SOFT SKILLS CASE #4: PREPARED

The career-ready class is practicing job interviews today. Each student is supposed to be prepared. That means everyone has completed an application, created a resumé, and is ready for an interview. The students take turns being employers and prospective employees.

Some students are prepared and ready to get the job! Others will need to keep hunting for a job. Who would you hire?

DO:
Investigate prepared successes and mistakes!

DO NOT:
Write in this book!

Who is prepared to get a job today? Who needs to get their act together?

WHO IS JOB READY?

PREPARED

If these were real interviews, which students would get the jobs?

Did you find all the successes and MISTAKES?

Start here!

Success!
Application? Resume? Confident interview? Yes, yes, and yes!

Mistake.
If ever there is a time to dress for success, an interview is it.

Success!
A good interview is a two-way conversation.

CASE NOTES

Are you prepared to make your career dreams come true?

Mistake.
Hello? Anyone there?

Mistake.
Freaking out in fear is not an option.

Did you find them all?

Success!
Nothing like a good question to keep things moving along.

Mistake.
Making yourself a bit too comfortable, aren't you?

Mistake.
Eating your lunch *during* the interview.

WHAT HAVE YOU Learned?

JOB SEARCH QUIZ

Question 1:

The Bureau of Labor Statistics reports that there are more than __________ categories of careers to choose from.

Question 2:

Getting curious about the __________ __________ can help you learn more about future career options.

Question 3:

Self-aware people figure out their __________, __________, and __________.

Question 4:

There is only one person in the world who is exactly like __________.

Question 5:

Brushing hair and teeth are examples of good __________.

Question 6:

People looking for jobs often have to fill out an __________.

Question 7:

A __________ is a tool people use to introduce themselves to prospective employers.

Question 8:

During an interview, you should be prepared to __________ and __________ questions.

ANSWERS

1. *800*
2. *real world*
3. *abilities, interests, needs*
4. *you*
5. *hygiene or grooming*
6. *application*
7. *resumé*
8. *ask, answer*

Job Search soft skills start here!

GLOSSARY

application (ap-lih-KAY-shuhn) a written request for something, as in a job

business casual (BIZ-nis KAZH-oo-uhl) a professional, yet relaxed style of dress suitable for the workplace

curious (KYOOR-ee-uhs) eager to know or learn about something

hard skills (HAHRD SKILZ) specific skills needed to do a specific job

hygiene (HYE-jeen) the process of keeping yourself and the things around you clean, in order to stay healthy

investigate (in-VES-tih-gate) to gather information or clues about something

job shadowing (JAHB SHAD-oh-ing) following someone around at work, to learn what they do

prepared (prih-PAIRD) to be ready to do something

qualifications (kwahl-uh-fih-KAY-shuhnz) skills or abilities that make you able to do a job

resumé (REZ-uh-may) a brief list of a person's education, jobs, and achievements

self-aware (SELF uh-WAIR) having knowledge of one's character and feelings

sleuth (SLOOTH) a detective, or person who is good at finding facts and clues

soft skills (SAWFT SKILZ) behaviors and personality traits people use every day to succeed in life

statistician (stah-tis-TISH-uhn) someone who puts together numbers that explain information

well-groomed (WEL GROOMD) taking care of one's appearance and clothing

INDEX

ABOUT THE AUTHORS

Diane Lindsey Reeves likes to write books that help students figure out what they want to be when they grow up. She mostly lives in Washington, D.C., but spends as much time as she can in North Carolina and South Carolina with her grandkids.

Connie Hansen spent 25 years teaching college students about successful life skills. She lives in Lynchburg, Virginia where her favorite thing to do is play with her grandchildren. Her happy place is the beach!

ABOUT THE ILLUSTRATOR

Ruth Bennett lives in a small country village in the heart of Norfolk, England, with her two cats, Queen Elizabeth and Queen Victoria. She loves petting dogs, watching movies, and drawing, of course!